HOW 1

Building Your Own Indoor Climbing Wall

Ramsay Thomas

FALCONGUIDES ®

GUILFORD, CONNECTICUT
HELENA, MONTANA

AN IMPRINT OF THE GLOBE PEQUOT PRESS

FALCON GUIDES

ISBN 978-0-934641-73-9

Manufactured in the United States of America
First Edition/Ninth Printing

Front Cover photo of Randy Leavitt in his home garage gym by Roy Silliker.

Acknowledgements

First, I'd like to thank Jean Marc Blanche, who taught me about making handholds and was an inspiration. His climbing sculptures in France are unquestionably the most creative in the world. The crew at Carp Mountaineering also helped enormously. Susan Merritt, Florin Botezatu, John Bakken, Simon Peck and Bruce Miller contributed experience and knowledge that has been invaluable. Don Miles turned me on to polymer cement, and that made all the difference. Bob Campbell developed many of the polymer cement applications used at Carp and included in this book. I'd also like to thank my family, especially my wife, Joss. Thank you all.

C O N T E N T S

BUILDING YOUR OWN INDOOR CLIMBING WALL

RAMSAY THOMAS

Introduction

This book is intended to help people build an indoor climbing wall. An outdoor wall can be constructed using similar materials and methods, but the elements such as wind and rain need to be taken into consideration. You'll need to consult an engineer regarding these special needs.

There are many ways to build a wall; some are fairly easy but most are rather difficult. The advantages of the type of climbing wall described in this book are that the methods are fairly simple, the materials are commonly available and standard building tools are all that are needed. This text is not definitive by any means. It is intended to point you in the right direction and give you enough information to get started. With the information in this book, and a little imagination, you can build a great climbing wall. The imagination is almost more important than the information, and that you must supply yourself.

I built my first climbing wall in a cow barn 20 years ago, with the help of a friend. We simply nailed pieces of scrap lumber to the end of the twenty-six-foot-high hay loft. It was crude, but to us it was the North Wall of the Eiger, El Capitan and Mount Everest. For me, a climbing wall is more than a thing to climb. A ladder would suffice for that. For me, a climbing wall is a place to dream and to play. For these reasons, it is important for me to design a climbing experience as much as a structure. I encourage you to do the same.

The Climbing Wall Industry Group of The Outdoor Recreation Coalition of America (ORCA, PO Box 1319, Boulder, CO 80306) has a constantly evolving series of construction standards for indoor climbing walls. These, in partnership with an on-site engineer, will ensure that the design you build will withstand the loads you put on your wall. Nonetheless, the building of the wall itself, while not extremely complicated, can be strenuous and some carpentry skill is needed. Get your friends involved, and most of all, have fun.

Where to Put a Climbing Wall

You need to find a site where climbing on the wall will not interfere with other activities that might take place at the same time. If your wall is to have an overhang and be tall enough to use a toprope, you need to plan space for a climber to swing away from the wall without hitting anything. High ceilings make for longer climbs. A sixteen-foot-high wall affords an opportunity to link together four or five moves vertically. Another option is to build a traversing or bouldering wall that is not so tall. While not as exciting, traversing lends itself well to training. Whether or not the horizontal dimension of your wall is greater than the vertical, the construction techniques are similar, so plans and construction descriptions can be used as guides for both. You are encouraged to let your imagination dictate the design of your wall.

DESIGN

Begin your project with a drawing. The more you plan, the easier construction will be. Often, you can uncover problems in the planning stage that would be costly or dangerous if discovered during construction. It is not necessary to draw architectural renderings from every angle, complete with shading and lighting options. A simple scale drawing should suffice. The scale 1 inch = 1 foot is simple to use, but you will need a huge piece of paper. One-quarter inch = 1 foot or ½ inch = 1 foot will produce a drawing that is of a more manageable size. These scales add a little complexity in converting inches to feet, so you might find it worthwhile to invest in a scale ruler, which is available in most art supply stores.

The scale drawing is an important tool for a number of reasons. It may be difficult to imagine what the wall you have drawn might feel like to climb on, but if you draw a four foot overhang and then take your tape measure and extend it four feet, you begin to get a sense of what that dimension is. Remember, you are designing a climbing experience as well as a structure. Arêtes, dihedrals and overhangs add immeasurably to the climbing experience. A flat vertical wall is limited and will soon lose its appeal. Even if you don't have the space or budget for a lot of features, a flat overhanging wall is still better than a flat vertical wall.

Once you have your drawing, you will need to figure out the materials you will need, and how much money your wall will cost. Often, the design will change based on financial constraints, and the drawings will need to be revised.

Elements of a Wood-Framed Climbing Wall

The wood-framed climbing wall consists of five elements: The underpinning, the framing, the sheathing, the climbing surface and the movable holds. As you read through this book, you will be presented with a few options for each element. You should decide which options will work best on your wall before you begin construction.

The underpinning is the structure that will hold the wall erect. This book assumes that you are using an existing floor, wall and/or ceiling as the underpinning for your climbing wall. I will discuss different attachment systems by which you can anchor the wall into the existing structure.

The framing consists of the vertical, horizontal and often diagonal bracing that holds the sheathing in place. Two-inch by six-inch construction-grade Douglas fir, or its equivalent, is commonly used for the framing. While 2x4-inch lumber might be adequate for certain limited climbing wall designs, it lacks the strength for most situations.

The sheathing is the material upon which the climber actually climbs. In this system, the sheathing also acts as structural support, preventing the framing from being pulled out of square by a climber on the wall. Imagine a rectangle torqued into a parallelogram; this is what the sheathing prevents. The most common sheathing material is three-quarter-inch plywood. There are differing grades of plywood; select one that has the least number of voids, the technical term for spaces between layers in the plywood. A plywood suitable for decking should be adequate for a climbing wall. Medium-density fiberboard also has certain applications, which will be discussed later.

The climbing surface can be anything from bare plywood to painted plywood to polymer cement. Features other than movable holds can be added to the climbing surface to afford opportunities to use different techniques.

The moveable holds can be purchased from an outdoor specialty shop, or can be made of wood, stone or resinous concrete. Each hold is fixed to the wall with a ⅜-inch bolt that threads into a T-nut fixed in the sheathing. T-nuts look like little top hats, and can be purchased at most hardware stores, or from a hold manufacturer. There should be many more T-nuts than moveable holds, to provide many options for course-setting. The subject of movaeable holds is complex enough to warrent a separate chapter in this book.

Tools

You will need basic carpentry tools to build the framing and install the sheathing. Here is a list of tools:
- Hammer
- Cordless driver drill with spare battery and charger
- Circular saw (with combination blade)
- Miter saw or miter box
- Hand saw (crosscut)
- Combination square
- Roofer's square
- Variable speed electric drill (three-eighths-inch chuck minimum, half-inch desirable)
- Seven-sixteenths-inch drill bit
- Half-inch drill bit
- Nine-sixteenths-inch crescent wrench
- Hex head or Allen wrench
- Ladders
- Climbing rope
- Climbing or rigging harness
- Ascenders & etriers
- A few carabiners
- A few bolt hangers (the kind used for rock anchors)
- Other tools that are really nice to have include:
- A table saw, for complicated sheathing such as overhangs, arêtes (outside corners) and dihedrals (inside corners)
- Scaffolding (for taller walls)
- A chain hoist (for larger walls with complicated sheathing, such as overhangs, arêtes and dihedrals)

UNDERPINNING

The structure that will act as the underpinning for your climbing wall is probably comprised of one or more of the following: wood, concrete, cinderblock, brick and perhaps steel. Whatever the material, you need to anchor your framing to it in a way that will be secure without compromising the existing structure. It is necessary to seek the advise of an architect, engineer or professional builder before any construction is started. A certain climbing wall project that I know of was never completed because holes were drilled into pre-stressed concrete beams without permission from the landlord. The drilling caused a potentially dangerous breach of the structural integrity of the building; the tenants were charged many thousands of dollars for the repair – and were then evicted. It is not within the scope of this book to cover all types of building systems that can be used as an underpinning for a climbing wall. I will describe the basic principles. You must be responsible for the wall you build.

Whatever the material, it is important that the connection to the underpinning be really beefy. It is my experience that money spent on engineering is money well spent. My designs tend to be beefier than they need be; I'd advise you to lean the same way. The ramifications of a structurally flimsy climbing structure are annoying at best and fatal at worst. However, my engineer has saved me money many times by simplifying my designs.

Although a great many climbing walls are anchored to wood underpinnings with lag bolts, I do not recommend this. Lag bolts, which are basically big screws that don't go all the way through the underpinning, eventually weaken and allow movement throughout the structure, resulting in the weakening of other joints and connections as well.

You need to anchor the framing to the underpinning at the top of the wall, at the bottom of the wall, and at regular intervals in between. You should follow the recommendations of your architect, engineer or builder recommends to accomplish this. Concrete floors can be anchored into with a masonry nail gun. Cinderblock walls often need to be through-bolted, so that the bolt goes all the way through both the wall and underpinning, and a nut can be secured to its back. Steel beams may need to have tabs welded to them, to which a bolt is attached; in some cases a hole can be drilled directly through the beam. Again, there are too many different structural systems out there for this book to responsibly address. Call a structural engineer.

FRAMING

A climbing wall's framing should be of 2x6-inch construction-grade Douglas fir, or its equivalent. But be warned, lumber dimensions are deceiving. For some strange reason, a 2x6 is actually 1½x5-½ inches. Adjust your measurements accordingly. Pick your lumber carefully. Look for straight pieces by holding the board up and sighting along the length of it. After you look at a few, you'll be able to tell which boards are straight.

There are three elements to the framing: The vertical boards (studs), the horizontal boards (plates), and the diagonal boards (braces). When you build an overhang, you will make what I call stud trusses. These trusses, or studs and braces joined together, have the profile of the overhang. The stud strusses are then joined with plates in the same manner single studs are joined in a flat wall. I will go into greater detail later.

The studs or stud trusses should be spaced at sixteen-inch intervals measured from the center of the stud, and should be placed so that the narrower dimension (the two-inch surface) is in contact with the sheathing. The studs are spaced so that each four-by-eight-foot sheet of sheathing material (a full sheet of plywood is forty-eight inches wide and ninety-six inches tall) is attached to four studs. The studs that end up at the edge of the sheets of sheathing are shared by two sheets (see figure). When the stud is at the edge of the wall and attached to only one sheet of plywood, the stud should be set in three-quarters of an inch so that the sheathing completely covers the stud (see page 6 figure).

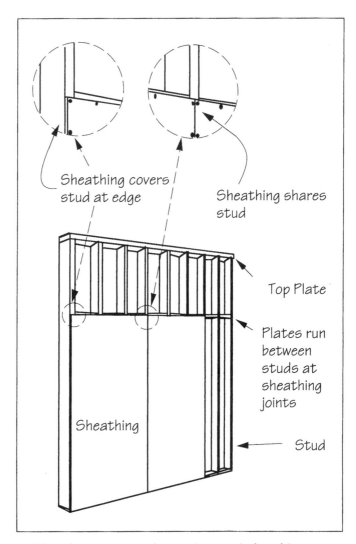

Sheathing covers stud at edge

Sheathing shares stud

Top Plate

Plates run between studs at sheathing joints

Sheathing

Stud

The plates occur where pieces of sheathing meet horizontally, and at the top and bottom of the wall. The top plate and the bottom (sole) plate run continuously across the wall unless the horizontal direction changes – for example, in the case of an arête. The rest of the plates run between the studs (see figure).

As with the studs, plates that occur at the edges of the plywood sheathing are shared by two sheets of plywood (see figure).

Framing a flat, vertical wall is fairly straightforward. Begin by anchoring the top plate to the ceiling of the existing structure (your house or building), using the method recommended by your architect, engineer or builder. Drop plumb lines from each end of the top plate, and make corresponding marks the floor. Using the method recommended by your architect, engineer or builder, anchor the bottom plate to the floor of the existing structure so that it is directly under the top plate. Next, using a level to be sure the studs are square, set the studs from the sole plate to the top plate at 16-inch intervals. Add the plates at eight-foot intervals, so that each piece of sheathing can tie into a 2x6 along each of its edges (see figure). The studs and plates should be joined together with three-inch self-driving screws driven in at an angle (use your driver drill for this). Be careful not to split the wood with the screws.

Framing Overhangs

Overhangs present an interesting framing challenge. Again, you build an overhang with stud trusses. There are some general rules about stud trusses that allow you to achieve both complex design and structural integrity. Within a stud truss, the studs must run continuously for as great a distance as possible. It is structurally unsound, for instance, to have a sixteen-foot tall section of wall comprised of eight-foot studs stacked on top of each other. Instead, use a sixteen-foot-long stud.

Studs and braces within a stud truss are held in place, at the appropriate angle, with plywood corner blocks as well as three-inch self-driving screws. The corner block should be made from ¾-inch plywood and should extend at least eight inches along each stud from the joint (see figure). It is important that the grain of the plywood used in the corner block runs across, rather than along, the joint. To join the plywood to the studs, a construction adhesive, such as Liquid Nails™, should be used in conjunction with the self-driving screws.

For the joint to be strong, it must be tight. The angles in the studs must be cut smoothly and precisely. A miter saw is a really useful tool here. Even seasoned carpenters use a miter saw over a circular saw for these types of cuts.

It is almost always easier, when building an overhang, to join the stud trusses together as a frame first. The stud truss can then be stood up on end, anchored to the underpinning and joined to the main frame with the plates (see illustration).

If you are building a really big overhang, you will need to support it in the middle. If you are using 2x6-inch fir, it will be necessary to brace any overhang with a span greater than 10 feet, and an angle greater than 120 degrees. If you are using 2x4-inch fir, or inferior-grade 2x6s, more frequent bracing will be required. If you are planning to lead climb on the wall, you should consult an engineer about bracing. Bracing can be made of either 2x4s or 2x6s. Long braces should be 2x6s.

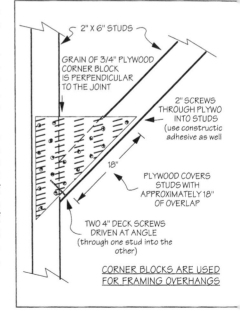

2" X 6" STUDS

GRAIN OF 3/4" PLYWOOD CORNER BLOCK IS PERPENDICULAR TO THE JOINT

2" SCREWS THROUGH PLYWO INTO STUDS (use constructic adhesive as well

18"

PLYWOOD COVERS STUDS WITH APPROXIMATELY 18" OF OVERLAP

TWO 4" DECK SCREWS DRIVEN AT ANGLE (through one stud into the other)

CORNER BLOCKS ARE USED FOR FRAMING OVERHANGS

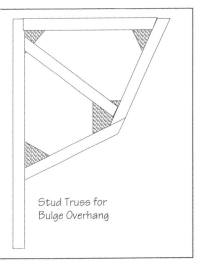

Stud Truss for
Bulge Overhang

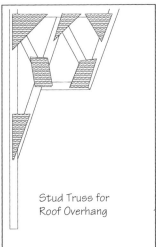

Stud Truss for
Roof Overhang

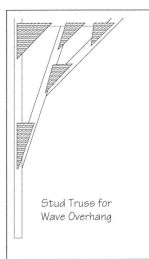

Stud Truss for
Wave Overhang

Ideally, brace will run at an angle parallel to the expected force on the stud. This is often perpendicular to the stud. The brace is connected to the stud with an overlap joint (see figure). The easiest way to do this is to hold the brace in place and scribe a line on it, using the stud's edge as a template. Bring the brace to the miter saw and set the angle on the saw from the scribed line on the brace. Make your cut, then screw and glue the brace in place.

Sheathing also can act as a brace. If your wall includes an arête or dihedral, the two faces will brace each other.

Overhanging arêtes are well worth the effort to build. They are a lot of fun to climb and offer a lot of potential variety of movement in a small area. Arêtes and dihedrals require a stud at the corner of each face. In a dihedral, this stud is perpendicular to the sheathing, with the two-inch face against the plywood, like all the other studs in the frame. Arêtes are not as simple. The best way to frame an arête is to divide the angle of the arête in two, and run the stud at this angle (see figure). If the angle is less than 90 degrees, it may be possible to use the same stud as framing for both faces. Cutting your stud length-wise at the proper angle will require use of a table saw. The plates will need to be joined at angles also; a miter saw is useful for this. Overhanging arêtes require that the corner stud also act as a plate for the studs that run vertically from the corner.

SHEATHING

The sheathing serves three important functions in the wood-frame climbing wall. Sheathing prevents racking, or twisting of the frame and provides the surface upon which a climber climbs. The sheathing also holds the movable holds in place. The sheathing material, in most situations, is plywood, which comes in 4X8-foot sheets. The plywood of

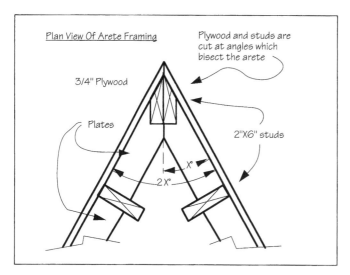

Plan View Of Arete Framing

Plywood and studs are cut at angles which bisect the arete

3/4" Plywood

Plates

2"X6" studs

$x°$

$2x°$

choice for most climbing walls is ¾-inch exterior-grade DX, or "rough on both sides" plywood. Five-eighths-inch plywood is sometimes used for climbing walls, but these walls flex when climbed. This is disconcerting at the least, but also means the wall is less durable. Three-quarter-inch is the recommended plywood thickness for a climbing wall.

Depending on what you plan for the final surface, different grades of plywood are appropriate. Walls that will not be painted or surfaced in any way may use AC or "good on one side" plywood. Hardwood-veneer plywoods are beautiful but are extremely expensive and would not look beautiful for long if used as a climbing wall. The plywood of choice, as mentioned above, exterior-grade DX or "rough on both sides". Even if the wall is indoors, it will be subjected to a lot of rough use. If RocTex or polymer cement is used as a final surface, exterior-grade plywood is essential. Stay away from

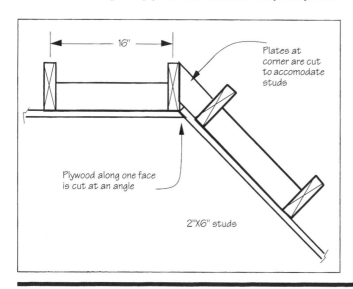

16"

Plates at corner are cut to accomodate studs

Plywood along one face is cut at an angle

2"X6" studs

particle board. Medium-density fiberboard (MDF) can be used in certain applications, but lacks the strength of plywood. Some surfacing materials supposedly can cause plywood to delaminate. I have never seen this happen, but Uniform Building Codes in some areas restrict the use of plywood with cement products. Check it out.

The simplest wall to sheath would be a single plane with dimensions devisable evenly into 4x8-foot rectangles. But this would not be the most interesting wall to climb. Design and space constraints usually require that at least some of the plywood sheets be cut. It is important that these cuts be precise. Mistakes in framing can be hidden with the sheathing, but sheathing mistakes will be visible to everyone. While the aesthetic considerations are important, there are also valid safety concerns. A simple fall that ordinarily would not slow down the fun could result in a trip to the emergency room if there is a jagged edge or protruding screw to catch the flesh of a falling climber. Splinters are a concern as well. The best way to prevent

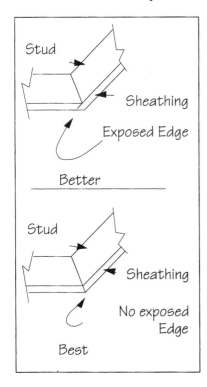

Stud

Sheathing

Exposed Edge

Better

Stud

Sheathing

No exposed Edge

Best

splinters is to surface your climbing wall. If there will be no surface, be sure to reduce splinter potential by using the proper blade when you cut the plywood, and by sanding where the veneer is chipped.

It is important to plan the sheathing carefully to minimize the number of cuts necessary, as well as the amount of waste. Plywood is relatively expensive, so plan ahead.

When the two sheets are on the same plane, each sheet protects the edges of the other. When two sheets of plywood butt against each other in a corner, it is important to protect the edges of the plywood. There are a couple of options for protecting the edges. If the corner is a dihedral, simply cut the edge of one sheet at the appropriate angle and lay it against the other sheet. If the corner forms an arête, it is best to cut both sheets so a clean, edgeless corner is presented. The above technique is also reccomended for the lip of an overhang. However, you could overlap the edge of the lower sheet with the upper sheet (see figure).

The sheathing should be attached to the framing with 2½-inch self-driving screws. It is a good idea to tack each sheet in place with only a couple of screws before the final attachment is made to see how well you've measured and cut your plywood. Once you're sure the sheathing is right, you can remove it, drill the hold pattern, surface the wall and install the T-nuts.

After the sheathing is cut to shape, the holes for T-nuts are drilled. The more options on your wall for hold placements, or T-nuts, the happier you will be. As the years

pass, you can accumulate a lot of movable holds and the more holds there are on your wall, the more opportunity for fun you will have. The holes can be drilled in either a grid pattern or at random. I used to believe a random pattern would give me a more realistic feel in my course setting, but I now feel that a regular pattern provides greater freedom. An eight-inch grid pattern is the minimum I would plan for my own climbing wall. If the grid is set four inches from the edge of each sheet of plywood, it will create a continuous 8-inch grid. This grid also conveniently misses the studs. If you decide on another grid, be sure to plan so you don't hit the studs. A T-nut against the stud will be useless and weaken the wall. Seven-sixteenth-inch holes are usually the correct size for three-eighths-inch T-nuts. Check with your T-nut supplier.

Once the sheathing is cut to the correct shape, with the correct edge treatment, and the holes are drilled, the wall is ready to be surfaced. It is a good idea to surface the wall after you drill the holes for the T-nuts, but before inserting the T-nuts. Otherwise, you run the risk of fouling the threads of the T-nuts with the surfacing material.

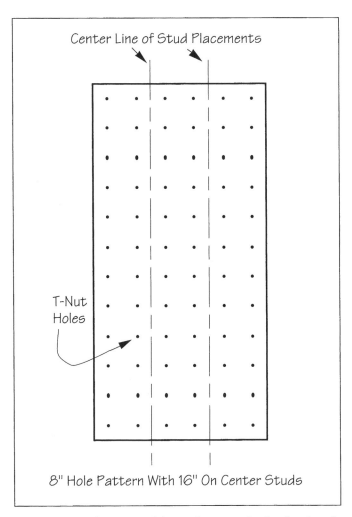

Center Line of Stud Placements

T-Nut
Holes

8" Hole Pattern With 16" On Center Studs

T-nuts are hammered into place on the back of each sheet. If you will not have access to the back of your completed wall, you should also glue the T-nuts in place. I use Liquid Nails™, but any construction adhesive that will work on wood and metal is fine. Again, be sure not to foul the threads of the T-nut with glue. Pound the T-nut all the way in and be sure the plate on the back of the T-nut is flush with the plywood.

Tack the sheathing back in place and check it again. When you are ready to permanently secure the sheathing to the frame, put in a screw every six inches or so.

SURFACING

There are a number of reasons to surface a climbing wall. The wall will have a finished look, which could be essential in a commercial setting but might be pointless in a barn or garage. But aesthetics are not the only reason to surface your wall. Plain plywood has a low friction coefficient; the climbs will be much more movable-hold oriented. With a climbing surface, there will be opportunities for footwork that can greatly enhance the climbing experience. Micro edges and smearability are well worth the effort if you plan to use the wall for recreational purposes. A training wall might not have the same need for an interesting climbing surface, so the climbing surface could be bare wood.

Small Features & Micro Edges

The first step in surfacing the wall is adding small features or micro edges. There are a number of ways to do this. The most straightforward is to simply glue and screw thin slices of wood and other material to the wall. On a wall I built in 1984 in the barn of my first house, we nailed and glued all kinds of junk to the wall. We had not figured out movable holds yet, but we loaded the wall with bicycle parts, broken gardening tools, rocks and chunks of wood. Knot holes in the plywood made great finger pockets, and a garden hose nailed down every two inches made for a lieback from hell.

On a wall with movable holds, the added features glued on under the surfacing should be very small. Let the movable holds give you the main course setting options, and use the micro edges as intermittent foot holds. It is important to leave space around the T-nut flat to accommodate the movable holds. A movable hold needs to sit flat against the wall or it may break when tightening the bolt.

There are a number of different glues that work well for climbing walls. Hydro-ester cement, the stuff they use to glue reflectors to the highway, works well. Certain epoxies are adequate as well. The glue must have strength as a filler, as well as a bonding agent, if the object being glued to the wall does not lie perfectly flat against the wall.

Apply the glue to the object and to the wall as per the instructions that come with the glue, then tape the object to the wall with duct tape until the glue is dry. If the duct tape is not sticking well, you can staple the tape to the sheathing.

Once you have enough micro edges on the wall, you can surface over both the micro edges and the plywood.

Paint as a Climbing Surface

Paints are fairly straightforward to apply. There are a lot of different non-skid deck paints available from your local lumber yard or hardware store. Many of these are suitable for climbing walls. If possible, buy a small amount of the paint and test it before you surface the wall completely. A texture that is too aggressive can be a drag, as it can remove a layer of skin each time you fall. On the other hand, if the wall is slippery you will be limited to climbing only on the movable holds. This is called dot-to-dot climbing and is fun about as long as connect-the-dot drawing is.

To apply the paint, follow the directions that come with it, being sure not to get any in the threads of the T-nuts, if you have already inserted them. Paint can really muck up the works; I once saw a wall built for a competition where virtually none of the T-nuts were usable because of paint. This was a little frustrating for the course setters, to say the least. If need be, get a bunch of ⁷⁄₁₆-inch dowels to fill the holes as you paint, being sure to remove the dowels before the paint dries.

Polymer Cement as a Climbing Surface

Polymer cement is a little more challenging to apply than paint, but is in many ways the best surface for a climbing wall. Polymer cement is actually portland cement with an acrylic additive that lengthens the curing time chemically.

Portland cement used as a surface for climbing walls can have a wide spectrum of results. At best, it has the feel and strength of limestone; at worst, it is a crumbly mess. The cement should applied with a trowel over the entire climbing surface. Small edges can be built up with the cement to be used as micro climbing holds, and the cement can be colored to look like real rock. It takes some doing to get the best results, but I will point you in the right direction and encourage you to experiment.

Cement was first used in ancient Rome to build structures that still stand today, but the cement-making process was lost after the fall of the Roman Empire and was not rediscovered until the middle of the eighteenth century. Portland cement, the standard cement used today, was developed in Great Britain a hundred years later. It is made of lime, which is either a refined limestone powder or ground-up sea shells (as was limestone a few million years ago), silica (a type of sand), and the minerals alumina, iron oxide and gypsum. For a climbing wall, the cement is mixed into a semi-liquid paste about the consistency of mashed potatoes. It is applied, and then it hardens.

Portland cement is a hydraulic cement, which means it hardens in the presence of water. This hardening, or curing, occurs as long as water is present. If the cement dries too quickly, it will not be very hard. The optimum curing time for portland cement is about 30 days. There are two ways to lengthen the curing time; mechanically or chemically. Mechanical curing means that the cement must be wetted down every few hours during the curing period. Sometimes portland cement casting is actually done under water to maximize the curing time. This won't work for your climbing wall because the plywood would warp. Wetting the surfaced plywood is questionable for the same reason. If you plan to mechanically cure the surface of your climbing wall, you should also plan to use ¾-inch medium-density fiberboard.

This brings us to chemical curing.

There are a number of acrylic additives available to chemically enhance the curing of portland cement. The acrylic is a liquid plastic that is used in place of water in the cement mix. If you were to pour some of the acrylic out on a table, it would dry into something like sandwich wrap plastic. In the cement mix, the acrylic coats individual molecules with this sandwich wrap and retains water long enough for the cement to cure. The acrylic also makes the cement less brittle and easier to spread, and therefore less prone to cracking. No matter how beefy your framing is, there will be movement within the frame as the climber climbs. The added flexibility of acrylic is thus a great benefit for climbing wall surfacing.

Since the cement is not structural and the acrylic is not cheap, you might be tempted to try curing the cement mechanically. However, getting good results with mechanically cured portland cement is very difficult. I strongly recommend using acrylic. You could waste a lot of plywood without it.

If you want the color of your climbing surface to be anything other than cement gray, or a muddy version of that gray, you must use white portland cement instead of regular portland cement. Colorant, the stuff used to make paint different colors, can be added to the acrylic cement additive to color the end product. A paint store should have colorants, although the salespeople may not be used to selling it by itself. Keep in mind that the acrylic, the white portland cement and the sand used in the final dry mix will effect the final color. With high-quality colorants there is almost no limit to the colors that can be

achieved. I have made walls that were bright green and purple. They were ugly as hell, but the colors were vivid. Mix a small sample with the color you've chosen before you commit all your material to a hue you may not like. Nice effects can be achieved using two or more colors of cement, which run into each other on the wall creating a marbleized effect. Go look at real rock to get ideas.

The dry mix consists of three parts sand to one part portland cement by volume when using the acrylic additive. Without the acrylic, the dry mix consists of three parts sand, one part portland cement and one-half part lime. The lime makes the cement easier to spread.

Once the dry mix has been sifted together, it is added to the acrylic or the water. Use a five-gallon pail – the white plastic kind used in the food and construction industries – to mix the cement in. You will need a fairly powerful variable-speed drill with a mixing paddle, and a place to mix where a spill wont be disastrous. Fill the bucket about a third full with the colored acrylic, and then add the dry mix as you stir with your drill. Keep adding the dry mix until you have a material about the consistency of mashed potatoes.

Wet the plywood with some acrylic or water, then spread the cement no more than a quarter-inch thick over the plywood. Once a piece of plywood is covered, you can go back and add the small edges. Depending on your material, you can build edges to about three-eighths of an inch thick. Paint the edges with the colored acrylic and smooth them into the desired shape. Be sure the edge is smooth; rough edges hurt to climb on.

There are many things you can do to improve on this simple method. Certain primer paints can be used, and a coat of portland cement and acrylic mixed thin can help bond the cement to the plywood.

I have been told that plywood could delaminate if the cement is applied directly; however, in the five years I have been building walls this way, I have never seen it happen. If you want to be really conservative, use the ¾-inch medium-density fiberboard instead of plywood as your sheathing.

One drawback to the polymer-cement method of surfacing a climbing wall is that you must wait at least a week to allow the cement to sufficiently harden before you can climb on the wall. The full curing will take about a month.

After the surfacing is complete, install the T-nuts. Be gentle when you hammer them in, or you will crack the surface. You can drill the holes ½ of an inch too big, and use glue to promote a gentle touch when installing the nuts.

BELAY ANCHORS

If the wall is taller than ten feet, you will need to install a toprope anchor. There are too many variables effecting anchor installation, and the anchor is too important, to be responsibly addressed in this book. However, a few words can be said. There are two kinds of anchors commonly used as belay anchors – belay bars and fixed anchors. Belay bars are horizontal bars at the top of the wall. which, to a certain extent, allow the climber to move across the wall followed by her belay rope, reducing the chance of a pendulum fall. There is the possibility of misusing a belay bar. The belayer must be attentive, making sure the rope moves across the wall with the climber. Otherwise, there is the possibility that when the climber falls, the rope will travel across the bar and allow the climber to drop. A fixed anchor is easier to use and in some ways safer. With a fixed anchor, the climber must follow a path that is pretty much directly under the anchor.

It is not uncommon to see static ropes used for climbing walls. A rope appropriate for lead climbing is called a dynamic rope because it stretches when loaded, cushioning the arrested fall. A static rope does not stretch. Some people feel that a static rope reduces the possibility of climber injury should the rope stretch during a fall near the floor. While rope stretch might conceivably allow an ankle to get twisted there are many compelling reasons to top rope with a static

(opposite page)

Randy Leavitt on his home wall.

Roy Silliker photo.

rope. When a climber falls with slack in the rope significant forces can be generated. The stretch in a dynamic rope absorbs a substantial percentage of that force. With a static rope this force is absorbed by the anchor and the climber. Repeated loads of this magnitude can weaken a climbing wall anchor but more importantly these loads can break a climber's back. Don't use static ropes.

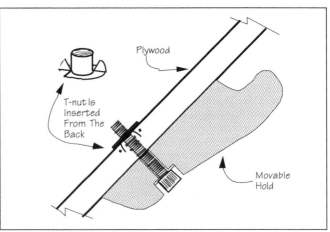

Plywood

T-nut Is
Inserted
From The
Back

Movable
Hold

Movable Holds

There is an ever-expanding universe of movable hold manufacturers out there, and the quality of available movable holds is excellent. The easiest thing to do is go out, buy a bunch, and bolt them to your new climbing wall. When you select your holds, consider what you will be using them for. For training, you will want a lot of big holds on a steeply overhanging wall. The texture should not be so smooth that your hand slips off them, but it should not be so aggressive that if you climb for more than a few minutes, you lose your fingerprints. The shape of the hold is as important as the size. I like holds that change in character when you rotate them, rather than simply being the same hold at a different angle. Small hold and holds with one or two finger pockets are fun, but be careful. I lost nine months of my climbing life to a snapped tendon due to a "fun little finger pocket." I was cranking off my one-finger lock when I heard what sounded like a pencil snap. It was about two months before I could successfully squeeze the water out of a sponge with that hand. Also beware of sharp angles. Holds should not be painful to use, nor should their use result in damage to your hand.

The main thing about selecting your movable holds is to get a variety. And, of course, the more the merrier. You cannot have too many holds on your wall.

MAKING MOVABLE HOLDS

If you are adventurous, you can make your own holds. Holds can be made of clay, wood, natural stones, or, like most commercial holds, of resinous concrete.

Making holds involves the use of potentially hazardous materials and manufacturing methods. Always follow manufacturer's directions on materials and use proper tools and safety precautions.

Stone & Clay Holds

Stone holds are great because they're the real thing. Select stones that have one flat side and are free of obvious fractures. You should can clamp the rock in a vise and drill a ⅞6-inch hole that will allow it to be fixed to a T-nut. Use either a hand drill or a drill press; either way, wear eye protection. This type of hold is not as cheap as it seems at first. You will go through drill bits very quickly. Sharpening drill bits is possible but takes a lot of practice, and drill bits of this size are costly. The end product, however, can be excellent.

Clay holds generally are the most brittle. They can be made using the techniques used to make floor tiles. I have never made these kinds of holds so you should seek the advice of a ceramicist. One thing that seems important with regard to clay holds is that the back be as flat as possible, to prevent cracking when tightening the bolt that fastens it to the wall.

Wood Holds

Wood is fairly easy to work with, is cheap, and does not require unusual tools. On the first wall I ever built, we simply nailed up the wood we found lying around the floor of the barn, and climbed. This is certainly an option, but there are easy ways to make more interesting holds out of wood.

In general, hard woods make better holds. For one thing, hard wood is less likely to splinter or split. Plywood is unsuitable for hand holds. Use at least one-inch stock to make wooden holds.

Wood can be cut into interesting shapes with a jig saw. A rasp and a belt sander are useful to shape the sides of the hold. Shape the hold so that one side is a sloper, one side is a positive edge, and so on, so the hold changes character when rotated. Remember, there is greater strength when loading wood along the grain rather than across it. Let the grain run perpendicular to the positive edge of the hold. It will be less likely to break. A $\frac{1}{16}$-inch hole is then drilled in the flat side, so it can be fixed to the wall. Finish sanding is important to reduce the chance of splintering.

Interesting shapes also can be made by gluing wood pieces together. Use a glue that is stronger than the wood. Most construction adhesives are adequate, or you can use epoxy. A rasp and sandpaper can turn any sharp edges left by a saw into smooth curves.

Wooden holds can be finished with the same surfacing material used on the wall. Paint or varnish can also be used. It is really important that the surface of the hold not be so rough that it is abrasive to the skin. Plain wood is okay too – just watch the splinters.

RESINOUS CONCRETE

Most commercial holds are made of resinous concrete. This material is made of sand, polyester or vinylester resin, and sometimes fillers like micro balloons (tiny glass beads) or glass fibers such as those used in making fiberglass. The sand and fillers are mixed with a catalyzed resin to make a thick sandy goop, which is then poured into a mold where it hardens. Resinous concrete can be made to feel a lot like rock, is relatively inexpensive, is strong and can be quite light. It requires a mold which, if you want to mass produce holds, can be expensive, but cheap molds that are not suited for multiple castings can be made with surprisingly good results.

Working with the resin is unpleasant and unhealthy. Precautions need to be taken to protect your skin, lungs and eyes. The resin will give off a lot of heat when it is hardening, so watch out for fire too. I set a dumpster on fire when I chucked out a bucket of resinous concrete that was hardening too quickly. The resin got so hot it ignited the trash around it. Luckily the only casualty was my dignity, and the fire was quickly put out with a garden hose.

Making A Mold

There are two ways to approach the making of a mold. The first is to simply create a negative space into which the resinous concrete can be poured. Go down to the beach, step in the sand, stick a ⅞-inch dowel into your foot print, dump in some catalyzed resin, wait ten minutes or so and you will have a crude but interesting hold. You can refine this idea, but the basic principle of sand casting has been around since the Bronze Age and it works well. You can also use clay, plaster, cement or rigid foam to create a mold. The big problem with a mold of these materials is that it is usually destroyed when it is used. You will have a one-of-a-kind hold, but that's cool – just step in the sand again.

The second way to make a mold is to create a model in the shape you want, and then make a permanent mold from the model. This is how virtually all the manufacturers do it. There is no great trade secret that makes this impossible for the lay person. That's why there is a new hold company every month. You too can be a player in the outdoor industry.

The Model

The model can be made from many materials, but the material that gives the best results is rigid polystyrene foam. Carving the foam is an art that takes some practice, but is ultimately easy and well worth the effort. You can find a dealer by looking under "Foam" in the yellow pages of a big city phone book. Florists also carry foam for use in flower arranging; some of this stuff can be carved into a model for a hold. Stay away from Styrofoam. The foam-cell size is too large for a good quality model.

I like to use foam with a density between three and twelve pounds. The denser the foam, the less aggressive or rough the surface texture of the hold will be. Begin by cutting a block out of the foam with a bread knife. The block should

Foam Modeling
1. a cut block of foam
2. Roughed out with a knife
3. Smoothed with a sanding sponge

Tools of the trade:
1. drill with flex shaft and "bullet"
2. other grinding bits
3. serrated knife
4. sanding sponge

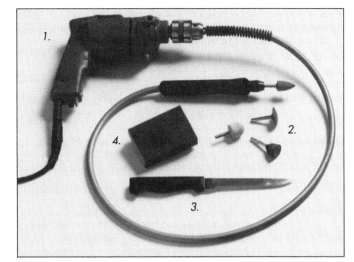

be a bit larger than the planned hold. Carve the basic shape of the hold with the knife. Using a drill press, drill a 1¼-inch hole into the foam, leaving one inch of foam between the bottom of the hole and the back of the hold. This is where the washer will go in the final product. Then, using the drill press, drill a ⁷⁄₁₆-inch hole through the foam in the center of the 1¼-inch hole. In the finished hold, the washer sits in the larger hole and the bolt goes through the smaller hole (see figure). Different washer sizes are okay, just plan accordingly.

Attach a flexible shaft to a hand drill and put a bullet-shaped grinding bit in the flexible shaft (see illustration). With this setup, you can carve smooth curves and square edges in your foam. Other grinding bits are useful for other shapes, but the bullet-shaped bit is the most versatile Wear a dust mask and goggles when you carve foam. The dust that accumulates in your lungs never leaves your system; it first

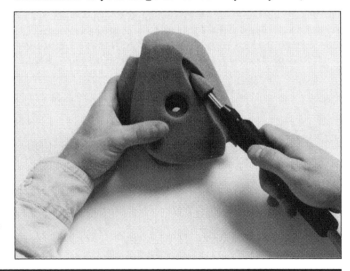

Carving foam with a flex-shaft and grinding bit.

does a number on the cilia in your lungs, then it moves on to cause kidney damage.

When the model is finished, glue it to the center of a piece of plywood about 10 inches larger than the longest dimension of the model, making sure the model is flat against the plywood. Using coils of oil-based modeling clay commonly called plasticene, build a leak-proof moat around the model to a height ¾ of an inch above the highest point on the model. The moat should contour around the model at least ¾-inch from its edge. Now, you're ready to make your mold.

The Mold

There are a wide variety of materials suitable for mold-making but the best reasonably available mold material is silicone. Silicone is flexible, so it can be stretched to remove the hold from the mold; it is able to withstand the high temperatures generated by the resin as it hardens; it can reproduce fine detail important to controlling the texture of the hold; and it does not require a mold release, which would also effect the texture of the hold.

On the down side, silicone is expensive; I have made molds that cost anywhere from $15 to $150. Silicone also needs to be well-maintained to prolong the life of the mold. There is a chemical in resin called styrene, which is especially evil to people, but also to silicone. A mold that is not washed regularly will become brittle and crack. Latex is an excellent and cheap mold material that works as well as silicone in terms of texture, etc., but it is destroyed by styrene and heat.

Mix up the silicone according to its instructions, and pour it into the moat, covering the model and filling the moat to the top. Gently but firmly knock or vibrate the plywood to encourage bubbles to rise out of the silicone. Let it sit still

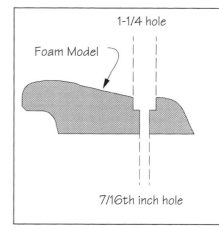

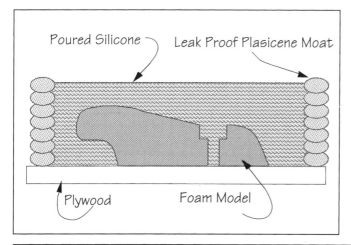

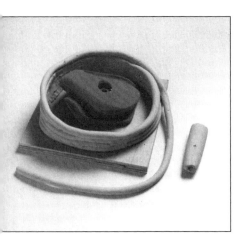

Laying clay coil moat for mold making. Silicon is poured into this moat.

until the silicone hardens (usually 12 to 24 hours). When the silicone is hard, remove the clay moat, then the plywood and the foam model. This will destroy the model you so lovingly carved, but do not despair. You now have a professional-quality hold mold.

The quality of the hold is determined primarily by the mold. However, the mix you pour into the mold also is important. The materials you use and the proportions in which they are combined will greatly effect the end results.

It is important that there be at least three different grain sizes in the sand used in resinous concrete. Play sand has many grain sizes and is too random for really good results. I like the three sizes of silica sand that I mix in my studio: # 20, #30 and #70. The medium and small sizes fill the gaps between the large-sized grains, and create a "sand resin matrix" that is strong. The proportions of grain sizes in this mix can be played with to obtain different results.

Casting Resinous Concrete

While the texture of the hold is determined by the model and the mold, the feel is determined by the material used as filler. By feel, I mean the way the heat and sweat coming off your hand feels as you use the hold. Tiny glass beads, called micro balloons, added to the mix will make your hand holds lighter but also will effect the feel. A small number of micro balloons will make the hold feel dryer, while too many micro balloons will give the hold an unnatural feeling. Holds can be cast without any sand, but the feel will be less than natural.

The durability and strength of the holds are primarily determined by the type of resin used. Many polyester and vinylester resins are available. Often, you can find a selection of resins at your local hardware store but be selective. Some resins are less suited than others for casting holds. You need a resin that has a high sheer strength and also high flexibility. I like vinylester resin, but this stuff is pretty hard to find. High-impact (polyester) resins are commonly available and could be a good choice. Buy the catalyst with the resin, and make sure they are compatible. The mixing measurements are very precise for the catalyst, so you will need a good tool to make these measurements with. I use a hypodermic syringe with the needle removed. Too much catalyst and the mix will "go off" very quickly and very hot. High heat will shorten the life of your mold. I have over-catalyzed the mix a number times, only to have it turn to stone before I can get the stuff into the mold.

The temperature of the materials and the room also will effect how the resin concrete "goes off." If the room and the materials are very warm use less catalyst, as the ambient temperature will speed up the chemical reaction. Humidity

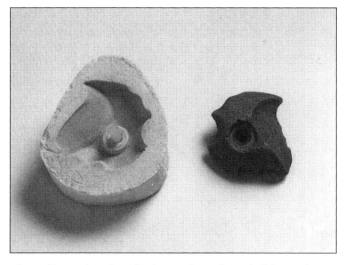

A mold and a hold.

also effects the chemical reaction, though I haven't yet figured out how. But whenever something really screwy happens, I blame it on "unusual humidity."

There are numerous recipes for resinous concrete that have various qualities. Here is a basic mix, and an encouragement to experiment.

For a heavy, strong, granite-like feel, measure by volume 33% resin, 12% fine-grain (#70) silica sand, 40% medium-grain (#30) silica sand and 15% coarse-grain (#20) silica sand. To lighten the hold and move toward a limestone feel, replace some of the sand with micro balloons. You can eliminate sand altogether, and even reduce the amount of resin, but there is a point at which the hold becomes too weak. This depends on your resin. Chopped glass fibers can be added to the mix to strengthen the hold, but at a cost to the feel.

As the resin sits in the mold, the sand sinks and the resin floats. This makes the surface of the hold more sandy and less resiny. As a result, the hold feels more natural, less like plastic. Chopped glass fibers inhibit the flow of the resin and therefore make the hold feel unnatural. There is no great mystique or trade secret to mixing resinous concrete. Have fun with it . . . play. But be careful.

When casting with resin concrete, protect your eyes with goggles, your lungs with a respirator, and your skin with a long-sleeved shirt and rubber gloves. Also, there is a potential fire hazard, so be careful, have a fire extinguisher handy and don't leave the house after you pour your holds.

To figure out how much resin concrete to mix, fill all the molds you wish to cast with water, then pour the water into a measuring cup. That is the total amount of material you will need, but mix up a little extra.

Remember to insert a washer into the hole you drilled into the mold before filling it. Pour or spoon the mix into the molds quickly and carefully. Once the molds are filled, they need to be vibrated to remove the bubbles. You can use a massage-type vibrator but industrial ones work a lot better. In my studio, I use a compressed-air driven vibrator that is bolted to the steel top of my casting table. The table top sits on rubber bushings, so it vibrates nicely. It is important that this type of setup be level or else the molds will dance right off the table when the vibrator is on.

When your holds have hardened, they can be removed from the molds. Do this with care to protect your molds, and wash the molds with dish soap and water after each "pull." Used a file to remove the bumps left around the edges of the back of the hold. If you have a table-mounted belt sander, you can take a few swipes across the back of the hold with this tool to clean it up.

Course Setting

An entire book could be devoted to course setting. I have been asked many times questions like, "How do you make a 5.8?" There is no simple answer. What I tell people is to play with it and have fun. Put a lot of holds up and then take some away, change this one for that one, flip some others over and so on . . . I like to imagine a sequence of moves, or some bizarre single move, and then build my route around it. Often, I find that there is another way to climb the route than what I envisioned, but that's part of the fun.